Love Songs of the Heart

Poems, Photos, & Art by
Vicki Kralapp

Ten | 16
PRESS

www.ten16press.com - Waukesha, WI

For information, please contact:

Ten|16
PRESS

www.ten16press.com
Waukesha, WI

Cover design by Kaeley Dunteman

All images © 2022 Vicki Kralapp

Special thanks to Chris Thorp, Linda Alcorn, Diane LaPlant, and all of my other family and friends for their help in editing and supporting me through this endeavor.

For Mom.

Contents

Introduction

My earliest childhood memories were of nature and walks in the woods with my mother, these and the poems of Robert Louis Stevenson, Pearl Riggs Crouch, and Edward Lear, which she would read to me. As I grew, my love of nature and poetry blossomed along with the trilliums and wood violets that carpeted the woodland floors in spring.

I added travel to my loves after our family took a road trip out west when I was a youngster. It was then that I made a promise to myself to see the world as an adult. Since then, I have traveled to many places and have had my heart stolen by countries such as Australia and Italy. But I only began to write poetry as a way to express my grief when my heart was broken by a different type of love: a love that was lost by the death of a relationship and the loss of my mother to cancer.

Mom always encouraged us to read books and write. Growing up, I remember reading poems such as "The Raven" and "The Swing," along with the poetry of Emily Dickinson, Henry David Thoreau, and other literary greats. I would watch her keep journals and write poetry to herself, and during the last years of her life, she would comment again and again how much she wished she could finish a book and publish. As I watched cancer ravage her body and brain, I knew that she would never be able to make her dream come true.

After her death, I began to hear my mom's voice whisper in my ear. And, as I began to grow as a writer and poet, I felt inspired many times. Often, poems would flow from my pen, as in "The Dream," which is found in this book. But more often, when inspiration found me, I struggled to find the correct words to convey what was in my heart. Over the course of a decade, I began to find my voice as a writer and poet. Many people during that time encouraged me to publish my writings, along with my photos and drawings. After nearly three hundred poems, I have decided to take the next step and make my dream and my mother's a reality.

This book is dedicated in her honor . . .

Words are the voice of the heart.
- *Confucius*

The Thin Places

You whisper on the morning wind,
amid the silent majesty,
and in thin places that I find,
I still can sense your energy.

A berth of solitude and peace,
beyond the realm of humankind,
where in the silence yet you speak,
above the din of all mankind.

These mystic places found on Earth,
between our worlds, the veil stretched thin,
where one can hear your whispered voice
and feel your presence on the wind.

The Snow Tastes Different on the Champs Elysees

I strolled this street of opulence,
where snow, it seems, tastes twice as sweet,
and distant smells assail our sense,
as music dances on the breeze.

An air of grandness fills this street,
with buildings dressed in twilight rose.
Aristocrats with wealth, replete,
are dressed to taste this evening snow.

Painting with Words

My friends ask me why I no longer take time,
to take pencil in hand, to draw what's in my mind,
or paint it on canvas, with a brush in my hand,
though I've tried to explain, they just don't understand.

So I simply reply that I now paint on a screen,
and I draw on a computer, with words and a theme,
I use what's inside me to bring words to life,
with a spectrum of sounds, they are just as precise.

Their only reply is, "But you're far too good!
You just can't put your art down! If only I could . . ."
Still they can't understand, nor could I in their place,
that the freshness of art has since gone with no trace.

Making art with pastel no longer conveys
what I feel is important, what I'm needing to say.
I no longer enjoy art's gestation and birth,
for it doesn't bring joy, only pain for its worth.

But the pen gives me strength, just as mighty as all
of the art that we see on the gallery walls.
Each image on paper, a picture complete,
is boundlessly infinite, each image unique.

There may come a time when I'll take up my brush,
when I'll paint what I see to the canvas I'll touch.
But for now, I'm contented to write what I feel,
painting pictures with words for the whole world to see.

Three Days in Moorea

Misted jade peaks tower above,
in a theater of tropical beauty surrounding me.
On a warm white sandy bed, I found my Tahitian tan,
as rhythmic waves drummed against the shore, lulling me to sleep.

At night, under the khaki canvas of a rented tent I hid.
Its sides sheltered me from terrors in the night;
long-legged spiders, alien insects, and falling coconuts . . .
I held out for the safety of my balmy beach bed.

Thus, I found myself at a time fate sneered at me,
as I pitched a tent under coconut palms,
along with fellow adventurers I happened upon:
Ivy League grads, a burly pipeline worker, and myself.

My memories, rich with the smells, sounds, and flavors of the Pacific;
vignettes of lush blanketed mountains, wrapped in turquoise seas;
and I, barefoot in the surf, dined on freshly cut coconut,
as I basked in golden days of the sun.

Dance of the Manta Rays

Within their world of azure blue,
the mantas glide on angel wings
and fly on winds of ocean waves
inside their realm of mystery.

Like ancient beings from the sea,
they flash and shimmer in our lights,
with otherworldly mammoth forms,
their curiosity takes flight.

These gentle giants of the night
draw fishes from the briny deep,
their vivid forms flash to and fro
while dining on the sea beneath.

They dance balletic in our lights;
exquisite turns and somersaults,
with bubbles lit to guide their course,
they glide just past our mortal reach.

These stunning visions of the blue
are but a finite sampling,
awaiting all who venture risk
beyond their scant imaginings.

The Family Garden

Impressionist colors rise from chestnut brown,
chartreuse necks stretch skyward.
Intertwining vines clutch each other in life's rhapsody
waiting to display their creator's palette of pure color.

Orchid and yellow chalices hold the morning dew,
christened in jeweled morning light.
Blue and white petals carpet the ground
blanketing hillsides in the hope of Monet.

Orange tongues of fire lick up towards the sun,
while jade blades battle with new growth.
Blossoms hang filled with a living harvest of gold,
awaiting transport to sister blooms.

Stalks of dried grasses stirred by August winds
dance to the rhythm of a warm breeze.
Summer ebbs away in aged colors of muted brown,
as life returns once again to muddied ground.

Broken

I marvel at this broken child
who's lived inside of me,
who struggled for so many years
and battled to be free.

To live a life unburdened by
those dark, oppressive years,
that made my youth a living hell
cloaked in unspoken fears.

My haunted past and fractured soul
could never quite recall,
the missing piece tucked safely back
behind its guarded wall.

So well my mind protected me
from all my silent fears,
that ne'er did I suspect what lay
behind my childhood tears.

Just like a ghoul, they haunted me
in dreams deep in the night,
and brought me to my knees when days
would spiral out of sight.

Then suddenly as if by fate
you've given me the key,
to open wide the long-locked doors
and set my spirit free.

Now done with anguished memories
that tethered pain to me,
I find that child within made whole
lives jubilantly free.

... For Molly

Gliding Into Aquamarine

Gliding through a fish ballet, in unison,
choreographed around arms outstretched.
Brilliant colors bursting around, leading me deeper
into this world of inexplicable beauty.

Bubbles dance, reflecting shimmering lights,
revealing the beauty of life unseen.
Crunching coral echoes from below,
while swirling stripes beat out the rhythm of the waves.

Calm and quiet surround, hypnotizing and entrancing,
entreating me to join this underwater revelry,
reminding me how insignificant we,
yet this world has existed in breathless eternity.

Growing Up Wild

Days of long, hot, steamy afternoons,
digging sandpit forts in the cool ochre sand.
Hunting grasshoppers as they flew from cupped hands,
I ran like the banshee I was, growing up wild in the country.

Memories of days in shorts and tees,
my skin stained orange with the sand in which I played,
living on Kool-Aid and peanut butter sandwiches,
sweet red raspberries, currants, and gooseberries.

Cool nights playing twilight tag with my brothers,
the air turned crisp, always ending too soon.
Lulled by the melody of country crickets and frogs,
we greeted sleep as our heads found their pillows.

Memories of
Life on Venus

You play your song
and I'm back once more
to a day of crushing goodbyes.
Sneaking in the back door
of my protected memories
you find me.

I struggle to hide away
from everyone and everything,
trying to hold back
the bitter tears
that flood
my eyes.

Collapsing in a pile
at the end of a wooded trail
at the ocean's edge,
my emotions spill out
in pools, like blood,
flooding over me.

A rock wall at my shoulder
and shells at my feet,
my tears overflow
as I sob through my thoughts.
Writing fails me,
and my words fall flat.

Even after a lifetime,
my breath still catches in my throat
to hear your haunting melody.
My eyes still hold tears
from the heartbreak
of goodbye.

The Dream

One night I had a blessed dream just after you had passed,
a dream about a crystal church, a place I'd come at last,
from a dark and dingy basement, through a hole that I had found,
a tunnel lined with precious gems, hues vibrant all around.

At last emerging from its end, I found myself a guest
in a crystal palace like the ones I'd seen from Europe's best.
The place was vast, so beautiful, and through the glass I saw
the brightest sea of spring green grass spread out from the far wall.

The air shone bright with shimmering light, like glitter dust it wore,
and all the walls reflected light I'd never seen before.
I turned to find me in the midst of figures glowing bright
like beings lit within themselves in pure and holy light.

The angels that surrounded me, enrobed in dress so fair,
were lost in joyful welcoming; they didn't see me there.
I looked to one I knew was you and tried to hug you close,
but you had not yet gone to look upon the Heavenly Host.

And though on Earth you were my size, you now looked down on me,
I understood, though nothing said, you'd somewhere else to be.
I watched as others led the way to a distant mountainside,
wrapped in celestial violet mist, they walked there, side by side.

New bodies they were given seemed to float along the ground,
a flawless, pure perfection given to all that could be found.
I stood there looking at the sight and knew that I'd been blessed,
and when I woke, I felt at peace to know you were at rest.

Much time has passed since this sweet dream, a vision from on High
was sent to me to calm my heart and say my last goodbye.
Though this it did, I still can see the angels and the hall,
a gift to see a glimpse of what is waiting for us all!

Beach Bling

Low tide,
at dawn's first light,
gently washes
sea jewels clean.

Fibonacci spirals,
surf waves to shore,
proof of
masterful perfection.

Frothing surf,
hushed by dawn's calming hand,
offers up its treasure
of nature's castoffs.

My gulf-side beach,
awash in Earth's infinite riches,
misty and serene awaits
as the last stars of night fall from the heavens.

Renaissance of Love

My heart is swept up in your whisper,
carrying my thoughts on a prayer of silent hope.
Your soft breeze caresses and warms my frozen heart,
lovingly embracing and healing my broken soul.

A lofty wind has taken me to your shores,
wrapping me in the sweetness of acceptance,
its mystical gossamer that healed these wounds,
reigniting this soul and lifeless heart.

Afternoon in the Park

A lone leaf sails on the breeze beside my bench
as the wind whispers her autumn melody in my ear.
Geese in flight overhead respond in their throated honk
as they herald the coming of an early frost.

Red-orange leaves drip from maples while all of nature hums.
Squirrels and chipmunks with their winter stores,
cheeks bulging with nuts and acorns,
scurry off in search of hideaways.

Fall, so vibrant and bright, enchanting all,
embraces me within this garden of deep contrasts.
I pull my jacket close against its crispness
and drink in the fading autumn.

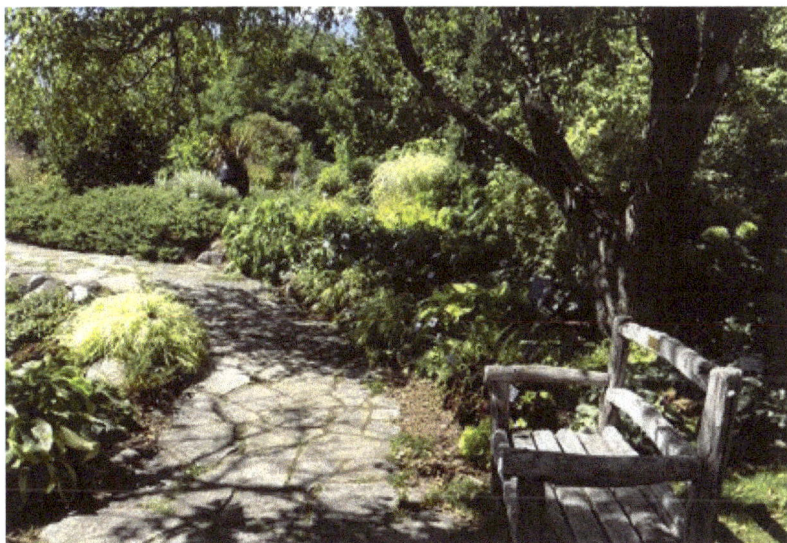

Awash

Shimmering light teasingly plays on liquid beauty
as the rippling blue slips around me like skin.
The waves consume and surround me with a brilliance beyond belief.
Time is but a memory; this world encompasses all.

Celebrating the palette of color gliding through its hands,
millions of tiny jewels bob and float as life takes a breath.
Treasures hide away, unwrapped with a stir,
while teams of blue swarm and dance about in warmth.

Blue-green shimmers with reflected light, glistening as it darts past.
Fans wave to the song of the tide singing with muted tongue.
Surreal and captivating, this world of the deep leaves me longing for more.
Isolated and apart, I return to my monotone world.

Maître de L'amour

A lover is like an impressionist masterpiece,
stroked with loving hands and
gently painted with grace by its master,
dressed in its finest, to frame the beauty found within.

You, my love, were like that master,
painting me to reflect the woman you saw inside,
creating a world for you to hold:
a ballet of colors that danced in your eyes.

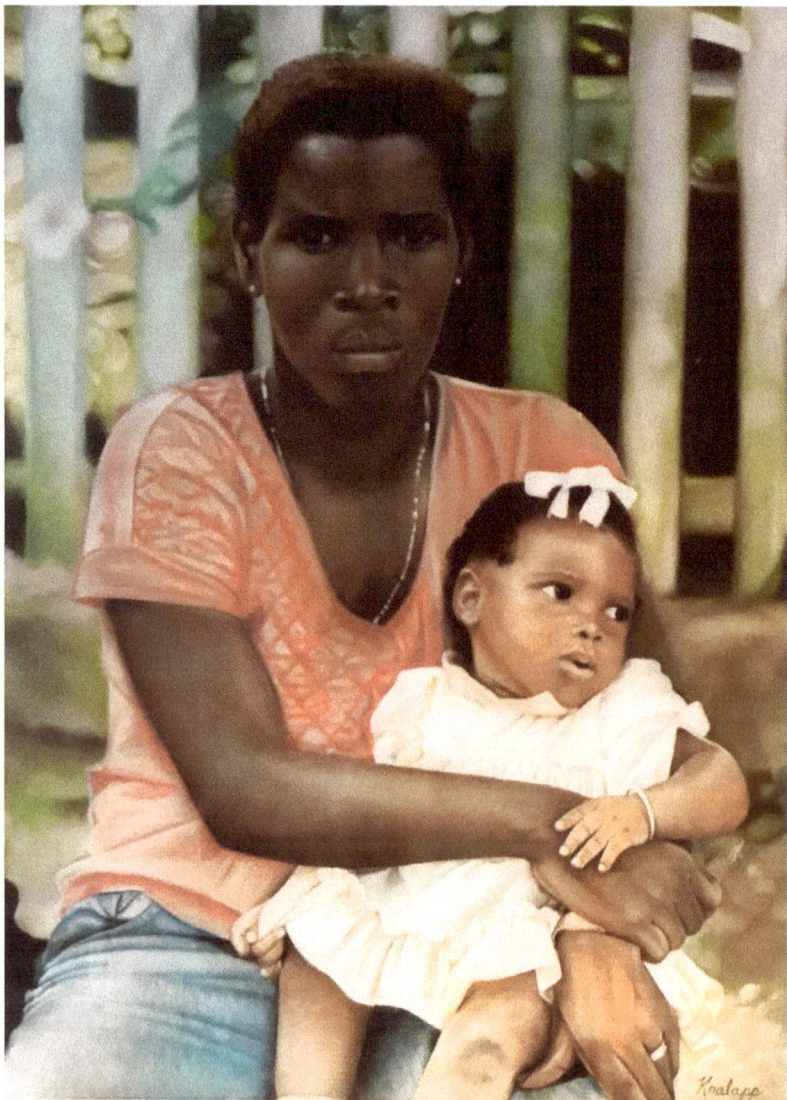

The Artist Within

Art, unborn,
aches to find form,
to manifest itself.
Within me it screams,
while those around
remain deaf to its cry.

It claws to free itself
from mortal chains,
restless to share its vision
with the world,
to tell its story
in verse and form.

This art within,
impatient, cannot wait.
It struggles to attain
its voice
within my world
of finite days.

Until at last,
like a volcano within,
unable to restrain its voice,
it erupts,
and art flows forth,
spilling onto paper.

The words and images
find form,
giving birth
to my spirit's art,
thus, completing me,
quieting the cry inside.

Footsteps
on the Moon

I've strode this graying, foreign land,
inviting me to tread its dust,
I've questioned why, this rugged path,
and why I've had to brave so much.

I've wept so many useless tears,
for heartbreaks life has thrust on me,
which left my journey full of fears,
tormenting me incessantly.

Yet, on this path of destiny
were hidden gifts I couldn't ignore,
in lessons that I'd hoped to flee
and silence which my strength restored.

So, with my feet set on the moon,
Earth's vision forms in front of me,
and I embrace this distant dune
where solitude yet keeps me free.

Visitation with Monet

Beside your cherished pond I sit,
with waterlilies of magenta and white
painted on liquid skin,
while dragonflies flit about its glassy face.

Strolling the paths you've gifted us,
you speak to me among the trees
and sing your great love song
within this vivid land of garden blooms.

Burning hot in the French sun, my neck cries for shade.
I find welcome coolness beneath your willows,
and through tears of gratefulness,
I savor the echoes of your spirit.

Summer Sigh

Summer sighs, its long last breath
hot and heavy against my cheek,
bidding me farewell before the freeze
as summer hugs autumn to its breast.

The Classroom Jungle

The jungle makes its calls, welling up from hollows beyond.
Wild things find their way through hidden spaces,
rapping on barriers beyond,
tapping as they mark their territory.

Sounds of birdsong fill the air, calling out to all too few,
while jaguars prowl paths in search of prey.
Packs of hyenas laugh while the jungle chorus grows
until the last bell rings and all flee for home.

In the Midst
of Dreams

Out of dreams you came to me,
a ghost of memories past.
You vowed to mend this broken heart
and help me heal at last.

But in the end, like dinosaurs,
a skeleton is all that remains.
Loneliness still holds me close,
you've just added to the pain.

I dream of a time before we met
and search for a path back home.
Why don't you leave my memory
and let me heal alone?!

Call of the Trilliums

My heart sings like a songbird,
in the warmth of early spring,
and soars to lofty heavens
upon a boundless wing.

It sings of each tomorrow,
in the hope of sun-drenched days,
and leaves behind the winter gray
and sets my soul ablaze.

It beats a vibrant melody
as we battle through our days,
and I revel in the bliss I'll feel
within the springtime rays.

So I await the tender green,
first buds 'neath snow's gray hue.
Its icy cap will melt away
and sprouts of life renew.

Second Summer

When summer makes its curtain call,
and warm winds die, just after fall,
before the winter ice storms play
and take their place upon the stage.

Your curtain lifts for nigh one week,
as autumn colors reach their peak
and dazzle us with one last play
before the audience turns away.

With one last act before the night,
of bitter cold and frozen white.
That final night, you give your all
and leave with final curtain's fall.

We wait then for next summer's end,
when autumn brings its lagging friend,
and summer takes its one last bow
before the last rich colors fall.

My Heart
Aches for You

My broken heart still aches for you,
I long to steal away your pain.
Your life now touched in shades of blue
and gray amidst the falling rain.

While moments yet seem as if surreal,
and energy has been erased,
allow yourself the time to heal
and wrap yourself in love's embrace.

So though your heart is bleeding now,
and pain surrounds your every bend,
your grief will lessen, this I vow,
and peace will find you in the end.

. . . For Emily

Hiking the
Old Sumac Trail

Along the well-worn winding path,
between burnt sienna sumac fruits, we made our way.
Their fuzzy felt heads brushing against our skin,
we basked in the rich ambiance of fall.

The smell of September's autumn air, clean and warm,
shadows stretched and long, in fall's Mannerist style,
painted dark on the green and ochre of fields,
from long school days, we played our way back home.

Rich days of golden sun on our backs, long and lazy,
grasshoppers and cicadas buzzing, guiding us along our way.
Memories of a simpler time and place,
when my young heart was filled with newness of life.

Life of
a Beachcomber

As I walk the morning beach alone,
with sunlight on my face,
I search to find these treasured bits,
in this still, mystic place.

Their bounty, seas give endlessly,
is tossed before my hands,
all wet with foamy surf-tossed brine,
shells glisten on the sand.

A dwelling once for housing life,
discarded now they find,
a special place within the soul,
with solitude of mind.

This quiet life of beachcombers,
we know it all too well,
need silence, peace, and beauty,
as we search for more than shells.

I Breathe You In

I breathe you in
like a heavenly scent,
like a day at the sea,
a Caribbean breeze.

School of the Seas

Beneath this world where life was birthed
is painted in awesome mystery,
Edenesque beauty fills its silent world
with creation beyond imagining.

Shimmery scales flash before my eyes
in the quiet of the afternoon sun,
as blue tangs dart in unison beneath
in the turquoise of shallow seas.

In a world pulsing with fresh life,
sparkling with newness,
it waits as we study its secrets,
finding infinite beauty in school of the seas.

Paint the Air in Autumn

Autumn's brusque wind slices its way through the remnants of summer,
painting maples in brilliant hues of red-orange.
Long shadows of late September streak across the last blades of grass,
as fall's stark contrasts light the afternoon hues.

The seasonal wind breathes cold with the smell of autumn in the air
while cotton clouds in a sea of cornflower blue slowly slide from view,
chased down by v's of geese as they race across the sun,
sounding their retreat before the snows of winter.

Helicopter seeds line sidewalks with gold, as others blow on the wind,
joining cones and acorns as they await the snows.
Crows, harbingers of winter, sing sad songs, penitent within their inky blackness
and the dark, cold months to come.

Squirrels pause to pack their mouths with fall's fare and scurry to secret caches,
their bulging cheeks filled with fallen nuts and acorns.
Fall greets me with a kiss as summer bows to its chill,
as autumn's brusque wind slices its way through the remnants of summer.

My Glass Heart

Red shards of this broken heart lie strewn about underfoot,
after a lifetime of war.
Once strong, protected behind walls of iron and steel,
its resistance rusted amidst abuse.

My heart shattered, I lie fallen before my foe,
vulnerable before Cupid's arrows.
I've felt their sting in the battle of love,
my heart, a tender puzzle now lies.

Yet, with time, wounds have been sewn,
as lead between stained glass,
broken fragments mended in vibrant hues,
while my light dances in reflected beauty from within.

La Dolce Vita

I dream of spending future days while roaming Tuscan lands,
where lavender haze hangs on every vine,
and follow in the paths of old, where artists' genius rang,
their echoes call from every nook I find.

In a world of ancient artists, where the Renaissance was born,
where poets and philosophers long played,
I'll stroll the narrow, crooked streets and walk the roads well-worn,
and live la dolce vita every day.

I'll spend my mornings writing tales, espressos at my call,
while I find the life of those in fairytales,
I'll stroll past art I've seen in books, amidst the hallowed halls,
and gaze in awe at David's massive scale.

Beneath the olive trees I'll dine, I'll drink the local brew,
while writing of my tales in verses clear.
And when my thoughts have found their voice, I'll bid addio to you,
with dreams you've spun to comfort through the years.

Morning Bird Song

Hope floats on gentle morning wings,
through windows just beyond the storms,
and lifts its voice in revelry,
within the willow's sheltering arms.

He joins the choir of morning song,
with harmonies that calm our souls,
reminding all to search beyond,
embracing nature's healing roll.

For now we seek a refuge
from our broken world of pain,
within the death and violence,
past ugliness that reigns.

So listen for the whippoorwill,
in morning's peaceful harmony,
reminding us that nature's gifts
are often gold we may not see.

Springtime Path

The warmth of life has come at last
to me along this springtime path.
Sweet fragrance drifts on morning breeze,
as colors dance on plants and trees.
While orchids peek from under pines
my mind drifts off and soon I find
myself recalling days gone by
and loves who always bid goodbye.

But while my past now flirts with me,
I take the time to let it be,
and make a choice along my way
to seek out life another way.
I still recall what's left behind
and in this heart will always find
a life that took a crooked path,
but now has found its own way back.

Time's given me a second chance
to see life at a backward glance,
and learn at last from past mistakes,
so with this choice a chance I take
to find another soul like mine,
and with that soul my life I'll find.
My heart has come full circle now,
from life through death a blessed whole.

If Wishes Flew Upon the Wind

If wishes flew upon the wind, I'd reach above and catch me some,
and bring them back to Earth with me, and keep them safe for years to come.
I'd wish for peace in troubled times, for those not knowing how to love,
and those afflicted by our plagues without the means to rise above.

For all my brothers in our world, I'd wish we'd all learn to embrace,
and look beyond our differences to see the wealth beyond our face.
For black or white, brown, red, or gold, we're all the same within our skins,
all look for love and brotherhood and truth beyond our earthly sins.

If wishes flew upon the wind, I'd catch a few as they passed by,
and turn my wishes into words to help those suffering as they cry.
I'd find my voice and sing with all, a choir that lifts beyond the noise,
and with this song, send up a prayer for those who hear, peace in our time.

Quietly Autumn Falls

Autumn falls quietly in the north,
creeping over gardens and woods
as she kisses the leaves in vermilion and ochre,
catching blossoms in mid-bloom.

The shadows of October grow long,
stretching over fields and hills
as their stark contrast reminds all
of frigid months to come.

Butterflies flit noiselessly about
from flower to flower, alighting briefly
in their search of nectar,
drinking in the remaining harvest of life.

A soft breeze rustles through the leaves,
bringing a shiver to my shoulders
as a solitary leaf sways with the rhythm of the wind
in one last wave to fall.

The Master Artist

Mere words can never quite convey
the majesty of nature's brush,
which paints the sunset's flaming rays
and pastel hues of morning's blush.

The whitened peaks which kiss the sky,
the mountain slopes that catch our breath,
are laced with orchid grandeur high,
and lofty clouds their crags protect.

The desert contrasts; stunning hues,
in reddish-orange of sunburnt sands
and skies embraced with azure blues,
are painted daily with His hands.

No one can capture nature's soul
and recreate its beauty grand,
for breathing life into our work
exceeds the skill of mortal hands.

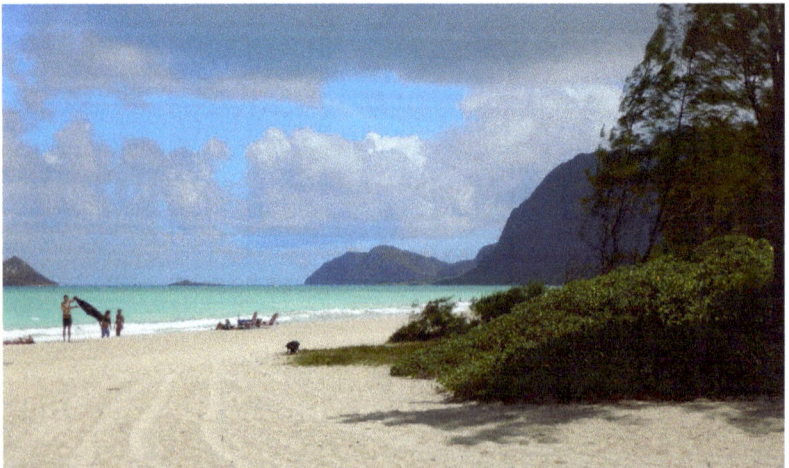

Growing My Wings

When I was young, no voice had I,
no wings with which to find my dreams,
to soar above my shackled youth
and find what lay beyond my chains.

Hungry for more, I ached to share
my art and gifts, what joy I'd found,
but found too few who shared the fire
that grew within my struggling.

But through life's pains of trials and tests,
a chrysalis of sorts was formed,
the life inside transformed to bliss
and freed me from my troubled mind.

Now perfectly transformed and freed,
I spread these wings and take to flight
and soar to heights I'd never dreamed,
before my life without my wings.

My Rainbow's End

I found my blessed rainbow's end,
amidst the autumn of my days,
beyond the shards of broken dreams,
that I have met along life's way.

No pot of gold yet have I found,
no magic spell was cast for me,
just joy beyond what I'd foreseen,
upon this path which holds the key.

I count my gold in happiness,
and dreams that have been given wing.
For I have found my rainbow's end,
in happiness contentment brings.

Island Memories

Pacific breezes breathe hot against my skin
as I swim in the humid air cloaking me.
Sapphire waves break against onyx sands
as we laze on our beachside blankets.

Among the algae plumes the seas explore,
a myriad of hues I glimpse,
brilliance darts on silent wings,
and khaki turtles bob on water's glistening face.

Fragrant plumeria wafts upon the wind,
its flaming colors peek through palm fronds.
Braided Ti leaves, offerings to Pele, dress trees
as distant lava illuminates the darkened sky.

Early-morning surfers balance on breaking waves,
while island melodies play, I muse,
and try to fathom its exquisite beauty
from everywhere I turn.

Running with the Wind

The humdrum of the day-to-day
never spoke much to me.
Its voice, foreign,
called in a language unknown.
It slept upon my porch at night
and knocked at my bolted door,
but was swept away each night
with every dream I dreamt.

Those many nightly fantasies
bore me on wings to distant lands,
reminding me to reach beyond
the only life I knew.
They coaxed me from this shackled life
to heed at last their call
as they beckoned
on the whispers of the wind.

So many times I've risked it all
and fled from all I knew
to follow my heart's dreams,
beyond the refuge of my world,
each time in hope to be
more than I perceived I'd be
as I run with the wind
and risk it all to be set free.

Secrets of the Moon

I've buried you upon the moon,
along with all my secret thoughts,
and hidden you away from view,
protecting this, my tender heart.

The secret lies we tell ourselves,
so ne'er we have to face the truth;
the pain we lock behind past years,
and desperation of our youth.

All banished to that world of gray,
along with anguished past released,
its darkness shading me from pain,
allowing me to live in peace.

The Great Reefs

Once I snorkeled reefs so grand,
their world alive in striking hues,
I gasped and stared in silent awe.
As fishes flashed beyond my touch,
sea fans, red and violet, waved,
I hovered just above their world.

Within pristine and magic seas,
life revealed its stunning beauty,
as clown fish caressed anemone.
Its sergeant majors danced on waves,
and darted past in prison suits,
with colors still vivid in my dreams.

In innocence I swam beguiled
by this yet unknown world,
its giant clams and bantam squid on display.
But now I fear I see more gray,
for our oceans are uncertain
and only draw a sad lament.

How blessed was I to swim within
paradise's deep watery garden,
yet far too soon we grieve her death.
And yet, we hide our eyes.
Her future in our hands we hold:
such gifts of Eden's deep.

Wind Chimes on the Breeze

You whisper your love song tenderly
upon the early-morning breeze.
You tease me awake as the wind plays its melody
through my open window.

Tiny prisms of light dance their morning ballet
on ceiling tiles above my head
in rhythm to reflecting shards of painted glass
tinkling along with dawn's breath.

This chorus of childhood memories whispers,
reminding me of life's beauty,
the fresh mornings of endless possibilities
each day sings us on the wind.

Colors of the Door

Stepping into the Door's crispness, just past the color's peak,
where the smell of smoked wood wafts on breezes,
I hike the paths and sidewalks of fallen leaves,
under trees, draped in yellow ochres and burnt siennas.

Lake Michigan, angry teal with late autumn wind,
rolls against the steel-gray rocks that hug its shores.
Whitecaps, balancing on each wave's tip,
surf their way to shore, crashing into breakwaters.

Winds whistling through the silver of leftover leaves
flit like whirlybirds reflecting the afternoon sun.
Feathered cattails backlit against the afternoon sun
line roadsides as they wave goodbye in the wind.

While the light fades in the afternoon sky, I pause,
delighting in the color and essence of October.
Turning, I bid farewell to fish boils, cherries, apples,
and views of majestic coves as I find my way home.

Winter of the Monarch

'Twas yesterday I caught a glimpse: a monarch in our bleakest month,
when blizzard winds gray snows around and buffet limbs left bare and brown.
It flitted past my courtyard door, on winds of powdered pirouettes,
which painted snowflakes on the glass, igniting visions in my mind.

I scurried out to glimpse its fire and dreamt of summer's sultry rays,
when frost is banished from our souls and green of life has sprung anew.
But as I caught a second glance, the image faded from my view,
and left instead was one dead leaf, reflecting winter's moonshine full.

Upon this phantom long I've dwelt, persisting through life's winter gray,
this lifeless form inviting hope, transcending life's adversities.
On nature's clues I now depend, reminding of my vision's strength,
and let the fire of monarch wings ignite my strength to soar above.

Taste of a Memory

Those lucid memories of early youth,
of warm summer mornings and sultry afternoons.
Hands, red with fresh raspberries and currants,
and sweet gooseberries round with ripeness.

Upon the forest green I lie, dreaming,
with open eyes turned toward the azure sky.
Beneath the cool of a paper birch,
painted green in full summer bloom.

Magic days of Kool-Aid, and picnic lunches,
and long walks through the amber September fields
flash before me, forgotten photographs in my mind,
sweet memories brought to life by your sweet taste.

My Tall Ship

Upon this tall ship, bound for life,
surrounded by the boundless sea,
its water-soaked and sun-scorched deck,
beneath my feet will ever be.

The main sail set, the helm I take,
and with my strength of steel resolve,
to let you guide me through the deep,
directed on this course unknown.

You've guided me to sunlit shoals,
set anchor when the wild winds blew,
and steered me to a harbor calm,
when all about turbulence ensued.

Although you've aged and changed without,
your strength of spirit remains within,
and I will hold to my tall ship,
while I sail the dusk of life.

Morning on Marco

The steel-gray misty foam, angry from a distant storm,
surrenders its treasures at my feet.
Bubbles and red tide paint its edge,
glistening as breakers battle with shore's sands.

Coquinas wait in ballet pose, tip toe in relevé,
as gulf currents wash them clean.
Sea breezes sweep across my face moist,
as the sun lifts its mighty head.

Sunshine Islands

The sun pours out its tender hues
over this land of hazy daybreak,
as cracks of muted chartreuse wink
between the buildings to greet me.

At first light, before the streets busy,
mist envelops the land,
softening the stark edges of man
upon this island, soft and lush with life.

Surfers atop swells that nod at the heavens,
their bodies silhouetted against the eastern glow.
I feel the surf's invitation at my feet
as I bond with this sunshine island.

Joy Upon Joy

Sad life, a doormat under foot,
in a world that saw only dust,
helpless to reveal her inner self,
she suffered in silent pain.

Knowing her life was made for more,
she spent her hours in search of ways
to rise above the discord and pain
of such an average life.

Her world was such a futile war,
a battle fought against her fears.
This feud fought daily with her will,
she searched in vain for peace.

Struggles brought her to this day,
to open the portal, leave the night,
and free what screamed within her soul
for all those troubled yesterdays.

Locked within those prison walls,
this little girl, now woman freed,
flown from the unlocked prison cell,
her own true spirit born.

For both the blessings and the tears
of all the long-fought yesteryears
have melted into lessons learned
for a past that's left behind.

I find this soul come spilling forth
and dancing gleefully about.
Today, I'm free to live my life
unburdened by the past.

Chorus of the Bush

The bush, Down Under, beckons me, and calls me from across the sea,
its sirens with their songs enthrall, with winged flutes and sorrowed calls.
I walk the haunting memories, while warm winds whistle through the trees,
and watch the ghosts of gumtrees play, while passing wattles on the way.
This foreign land bewitches me, and to my heart it holds the key,
a land where once my spirit played, the home from whence I've long delayed.

At once I knew your foreign shore, as if I'd lingered there before,
its memories haunt, reminding me of golden grasses by the sea,
within a voice I can't ignore, with whispers, "You've been here before!"
This vision in my mind foreseen? Just déjà vu? I can't concede.
But this has opened wide a door, a memory floodgate from your shore.
Another life across the sea? Has made a curious memory.

When darkness flees, and morn is new, when laughter bids the night adieu,
then bellbirds ring the morning in, their chimes float on the early wind.
Where rainbow lorikeets accrue, and birds arrayed in nature's hues.
The bushland floor, dressed in the marks of gum nuts, leaves, and paperbark,
along with virgin bushland too, when all of nature sang anew,
the master painter here has been, as seen in beauty from within.

As dark recedes and light breaks through, all glisten in the morning dew,
then sunlight paints upon its face: to paperbarks and banksias,
the bottlebrush and wattle hues, all readied for the day's review.
Loud kookaburras' raucous calls, with cockatoos and pink galahs,
pied currawong and magpie flutes, enchanting with their morning lutes,
all joined in bushland's magic call, and with their song, I am enthralled.

I've been across this curious land, and seen more than I may have planned,
from Alice Springs and Uluru, and Darwin north of Kakadu,
the Barrier Reef, near gateway Cairns, and Sydney with its city grand.
But 'tis the bush I can't forget; with nature's jewels its land beset,
and calls that pique my memory and wilderness that set me free,
my heart counts every day anew and longs to bring me back to you.

Inside This Winter's Storm

Upon this dark and snow-filled sky,
I gaze out past the city's glow,
at snowflakes flying past the lights
that blanket all that lie below.

On such a winter's night as this,
awaiting sleep, both deep and fast,
within the midst of icy winds
and winter's polar vortex blast.

A mug of cocoa at my lips,
I warm my hands upon its sides,
and bid the gale winds hasten through,
while in my gray room now I hide.

I lie beneath my downy quilt,
and curl up with a classic tale,
as storm winds howl with mighty force,
I shelter from this stormy gale.

The Mighty Sea

The mighty sea, majestic rolls,
with strength beyond our mortal realm,
within that awesome mystery,
the breath of life still dwells within.

Its furled waves roll cresting high,
and buffet while the wild winds rage.
Within its depths, adventure thrives,
and beckons to the wild in me.

I watch enchanted by her soul,
adventure's deepness undenied,
her spirit ever rolls beneath,
and I, in fearless awe, abide.

Grains of Sand

Grains of sand upon love's shores
have called me back to life once more,
ignited by the fantasies
of palm trees in my memories.

With sweetened kisses in the sand,
and dances to a reggae band,
along with loving friends who shared
the sweetest days that life could bear.

Although now life is not the same
as what I'd known before the pain
of love tossed out by carelessness
and friendship lost without bequest.

But life will not keep this one down,
I'm ready for another round
of trusting time and fate's command,
to quiet pain with loving hands.

Now love can play its hand again,
and take me to that southern land,
where days are filled with endless glee,
of joy that sets my spirit free.

So when that music calls to me,
at last, for freedom just to be,
with grains of sand between my toes,
I have, at last, found me at home.

My Ode to Joy

My heart sings like a songbird,
in the warmth of early spring,
and soars to lofty heavens
upon an open wing.

It sings of each tomorrow,
with hope of sun-drenched days,
and leaves behind the frostiness
of polar vortex waves.

It beats a vibrant melody,
with dreams of balmy days,
as I revel in the bliss I'll feel
when summer's starlight plays.

So I await the tender green,
beneath the graying cold,
which winter's quilt restrains within
its shell of crusty snow.

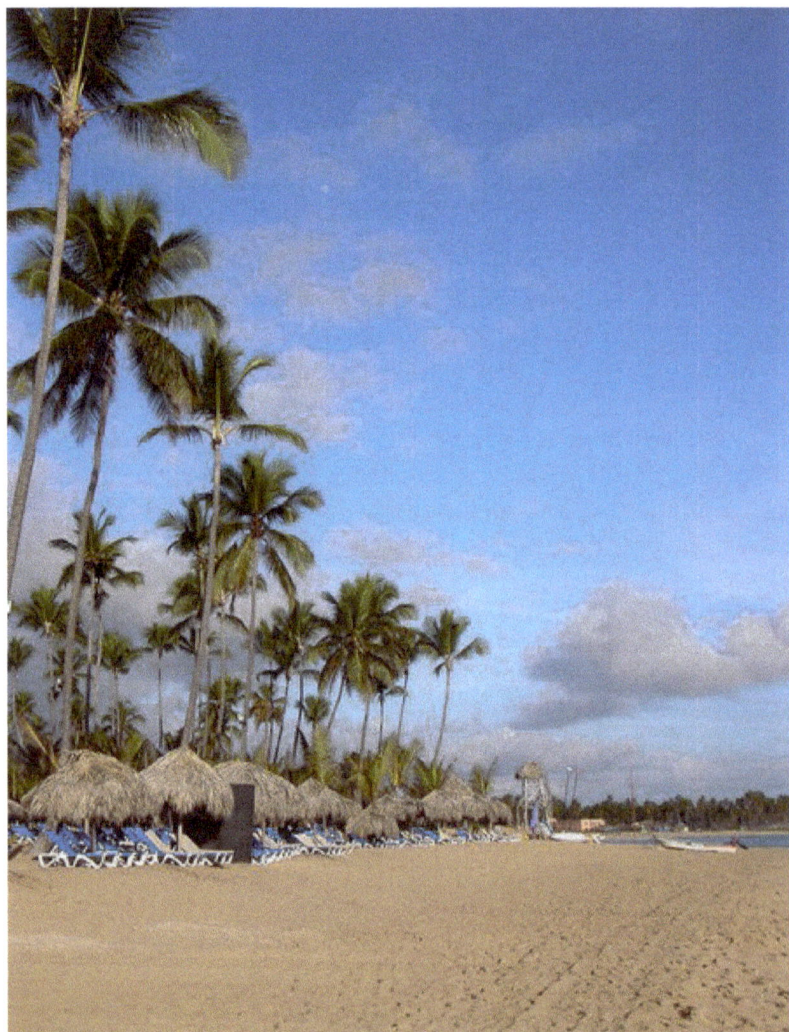

Through My Camera's Lens

Our world speeds past our eyes unseen,
as if through empty windowpanes,
yet I have paused this life to catch
its brilliance with my camera's lens.

The changing colors of the trees,
when autumn tips its leaves in flame,
the grandeur of majestic seas,
and brilliance of this stunning land.

Within the cityscapes it seeks
amazing artistry to find
inside art galleries and halls
with every photo found therein.

These captured for my aged self
to fill those empty panes with joy
recalling sweetened memories
of this life which has overflowed.

Twisted Art

We glide through life on hollow wings, while making art with earthly things,
when halting beauty stops us all around.
Unmindful of the world we share and bounty we are gifted here,
content to fool ourselves with pleasures found.

We search in vain like fools to find a beauty of a special kind,
our voices plead for all the world to see,
how wonderful our talents are, to spread our names and stories far
and grant our memories live enduringly.

How foolish to believe we can, along with czars and magic men,
light fires so grand to burn eternally.
When most our hopes and dreams can bear is priceless bliss in moments shared,
with cherished souls and gifts we're given free.

Standing on Kryptonite

You've made me believe with you I can fly
and reach for the stars as they pass by.
You carry me past galaxies floating on clouds,
wrapped in my dreams and loving out loud.

The magical carpet that sweeps me away
leaves me helpless and breathless, just wanting to stay
on Kryptonite, that mystic existence beyond,
where time does not matter and magic abounds.

On top of a mountain, a planet beyond,
I cling to your safety and hold to your calm.
Should I speak of the beauty that you have shown me?
The doors you have opened, the wonders I see?

My lips cannot form the words now in my mind,
the heaven you've brought, the expressions now hide.
Before you appeared in my life, it was full,
yet my days seemed so barren, bereft of a soul.

I traveled through life, all alone without you,
now you've come to my rescue, in your red and your blue.
I gaze at the others who have been here before,
look back at their lives to all theirs had borne.

I smile at their journeys, as they'll never know,
for the heavens I've reached on my ride do not show.
The best of the journey is yet to explore,
as I take to the skies on my carpet once more.

I stand here with Superman close by my side
on the mountain of Kryptonite ready to ride.

Waiting for Spring

Waiting for spring this winter's day,
straining to touch the warmth of memories past.
Caught in this prison of frosted white and gray
longing to break these frozen chains.

Remnants of fall, crumpled about like brown paper,
drab beige grass poking through snow, sucking it dry.
Freeze-dried fruit fallen against twisted roots,
while overhanging limbs and stalks drip with liquid glass.

Winter birds cling to gray, lifeless branches,
crying out in their search of winter's fare.
Animal tracks dot the landscape in patchwork quilts,
its white powder etched in waves lead off to their crusty end.

Sparse, sun-filled days bring brief glimpses of hope.
The promise of warmth waits to banish the frigid cold
that holds me to this land and existence,
as I await spring to thaw this soul.

Dante's Shores

We've left the safe too far behind
and crossed the flood to darkened shores,
to build our homes within its thorns
and lies that have ensnared us all.

We've ransomed our souls for our desires,
their blackness branded on our hearts
that blinds us to what matters most
as future dreams still fade.

While truth and decency have flown,
we've given up the ground we've gained,
and hide behind our secret walls
whilst past mistakes replay.

With guarded hearts and shuttered minds,
the world we watch moves forth unseen;
we have the chance to change it all
while we sleep on Dante's shores.

Water's Edge

The smell of coffee wafts above the saltwater sprays,
while I daydream my afternoon away.
Tall ships sail by, I drink in the ambience of this moment
overtaken by memories, I drift back in time.

I'm back in the harbor, on that sunlit afternoon
of your bicentennial birthday jubilee.
Wringing every drop from those blissful days,
I held to this new world with each step.

Discovering myself awakening through new eyes,
maturing, becoming my own.
Like family, you've been my mentors and friends
as you've helped me traverse the fires of life.

Morning teas, sunrise chats, and hikes on the beach,
time cementing friendships along the way.
Watching dolphins at dawn on the Central Coast shores,
a sense of belonging across seasons and seas.

My life came undone when I first saw your land,
my heart crushed with our first goodbye,
and that bond kept me spellbound,
forever transforming this pilgrim and view of her world.

Dream Catcher

I reached to catch my silent dreams
that teased me in my sleep
of distant lands beyond my grasp
and freedom to be me.

So many times I wished that I
could just forgo this fight,
long days of solitude and grief
and battling through my nights.

Blind to the gifts that lay within
and strengths inside concealed,
I struggled while my broken heart
refused to let me heal.

But now I'm filled with thankfulness,
for lessons life taught me,
as I tightly hold those hard-won gifts
that caught these dreams for me.

Watching the Springtime Melt

Fingers of ice cry from the eves,
as tears drip on muddy ground.
Rivulets whirl down ravines in springtime frolic,
before dancing from sight.

Banks of cotton candy snow begin to thaw
as last year's grass, brown with age,
struggles within its sarcophagus of gray
through the last gasp of snow.

Melody of Life

My song, a melody composed
on tender strings each passing day.
This ballad's mine, and mine alone,
a verse of life to sing my way.

'Tis never plain and seldom free,
with hidden trials in each refrain.
Its lyrics are my battle song,
within its verse my spirit strains.

The songs that I've sung through life,
at last, have finally found their sound:
a voice of hope, in aging years,
in solo a cappella found.

While traveling through this fleeting life,
I lift my voice the world to hear
and sing my life upon the wind
in passions that I hold so dear.

*For all of my friends still searching
for their voices...*

Vicki Kralapp is also a published
author of the self-help book,
My Time to Sing, and
holds a degree in Fine Art
with certificates in both
teaching and tourism.

www.ingramcontent.com/pod-product-compliance
Lightning Source LLC
LaVergne TN
LVHW070013090426
835508LV00048B/3387